A Tale of an Intelligent Psychopath

Based on a true story

Josephs Quartzy

ISBN 978-93-5610-506-5

Published in India 2022 by Pencil

A brand of
One Point Six Technologies Pvt. Ltd.
123, Building J2, Shram Seva Premises,
Wadala Truck Terminal, Wadala (E)
Mumbai 400037, Maharashtra, INDIA
E connect@thepencilapp.com
W www.thepencilapp.com

Author biography

Joseph Marwa proffesionally known as Josephs Quartzy is a Tanzanian singer-songwriter, actor and author

CONTENTS

The Village 7
A Heartbreaking Tale 11
Intelligent Kid Comes 15
Unintentionally Marriage 19
The Psychopath 23
A Root of All Evils 27
Dumped 31
A Dim Survival 35
New Life, New Beginning 39
Road to Prosperity 43
Polygamous Hell 47
Downfall 51
Great Strike 58
Where Did everyone Go 63
Morals 67

Acknowledgements

Since God gave me brain, health, and breathing, He gave me much more than anything or anyone else, I would love to thank Almight God for the love and grace he has always shown me, my family, neighbours and to all his children around the world.

My sincere thanks go to everyone who has helped me on one way or the other on assisting me on anything I needed, especially time to complete this beautiful book of mine.

1. Asma Sadick Mkombo
2. Alex Johnson Jordan
3. Johnas Marcus
4. Pateick Musela
5. Nyambita Magoma
6. Bongo Times Family &
7. My beautiful Family

Introduction

"My name is Mara Jean Mara or simply Mara Jr, ooh…! I have a modern name too, sometimes friends call me 'Joe' though it is actually an abbreviation or a slang name for my full name José, I love it kept that way. In this modern and civilized world, how would I dare to miss a cool modern name?……. I'm actually a college graduate and since I'm still jobless, I sometimes get time to settle down, grab a pen and a notebook and remember whatever happened and still happening in my life (sometimes friends' daily lives) and note them down, at last I find that whatever a story I've written makes a full novel.

I'm best known to be the eldest male grandson of the great Mr. Mara and Anna also the firstborn of Jean and Aggie who will be the main characters on this beautiful novel I would love to share with you.

The story is all about my family including my parents fantasies, my culture and so much more that you will love and learn from.

Though the story may be full of sad moments, funny and seems to be too long sometimes, I hope you will love and enjoy something, Let's dive in……….

The Village

Kyawaza is a pastoral village found in Tanzaland only a few kilometers from Madarak, a small nearby famous trading center. Kyawaza is occupied mostly by people of Kurya tribe and some other small tribes of Zanaki, Jita, Simbiti, Kerewe and much more that I could never have a chance to claim their names.

Though Kyawaza seems to be the best place for animals to live in and tourists to visit and enjoy because of it's natural forests, plenty seasonal rains, waterfalls, and much more, Kyawaza is the hell village for a modern and civilized humans to live in because Kyawaza has almost none of human basic and essential needs such as electicity, water supply, hospitals, schools or even proper roads to walk on. One is required to arrage a proper miles walk if he or she plans to get them. Also Kyawaza is occupied by highly illiterate rate that, inhabitants of the village still have unwanted local beliefs, cultures and customs such as women circumcision, women beatings and females are never allowed to attend to schools to be educated since they are treated as properties.

Kyawaza's dwellers are both circumcised per Kurya's customs, means both men and women are required to be circumcised no matter the circumstances (though this seems to be taken care of by government, NGO's and some other good people), because circumcision was the highest level of respect in Kurya's community right after riches and power.

In today's world, circumcision to male is a normal norm to alot of communities around the world, even the Healthcare proffesionals would advice a man to have it to keep his healthy much more safer, but Kurya's style of circumcision would leave people staring.

If I wouldn't take much of your time I can expain how it is done; firstly, it is done to only the grown-up men, children are considered as weak and cannot bear so much pain, and circumcision ceremony is the biggest of all Kurya ceremonies because it comprises of alot of clans from different villages and it is done only once a year. It is a ceremony that a family or a clan add much more warriors and manpower to their households (this means anyone who is circumcised is officially upgraded into a warrior and a real man is even ready to marry, these are called 'Mbhamura' while uncircumcised are called 'Mbharisya' which is the slammest name of all). The whole process of circumcision is done by only one person holding a single knife that does all the circumcision to the boys and older men standing in line sorrounded by thousands of already circumcised men and women. Every person in line is asked the about duration he would love to be circumcised, the strongest would make their families proud by requesting a very long time up to three hours (here a circumciser is cutting only a small part of a skin that is required to be removed then continue to other boys, he would eventually return sometimes and as before, he would cut another small portion of it, the circumciser will repeat the same step untill the mentioned duration is over even if it is three hours) and others would request only a minute (here a circumciser cuts a part that is required to be removed in only one go and the work is done).

A boy is then given alot of gifts because of his bravery some get themselves rewarded thousands of cows, goats, sheeps, birds, money and other presents, he also receives a private family party. The fun fact about the money rewarded is that, not even a single coin of that money is supposed to be used for development purposes, they should be spent for them to be finished no matter how much the amount is.

I never had a chance to witness females circumcised so I'm really sorry because I would not talk about.

****

Mr. Mara, a retired army officer notable for his wickedness, rudeness, and cruelty is the chairman of Kyawaza village for a 40th year now and has no intention of stepping down, it seems now only death can take over his throne.

Though Mr. Mara seems to be a bad person, everyone in the village respect and adore him.

The basic questions remain how could a person of his calibre be a leader? How would everyone respect a person with such behaviors? How would someone with common senses respect him?

Mr. Mara have had a controversial and confusing lifestyle that anyone would stare and remain still holding a breathe for a moment after hearing or witnessing it all.

Sometimes he would act like a wise person, sometimes he would act like a mad man and he would even injure or cripple someone because of just a very simple mistake. I can clearly recall a story told by his sons that one of his sons Called Mamba once talked back to him in a bad manner that he didn't like, all he had to do was going inside, taking out his gun pointing at the same direction as Mamba was running, he truly pulled the trigger and was ready to kill his own son but goodluck is born within people, Mamba slipped and bullet shot aside.

****

Mara Jose Nyamambya referred shortly as Mr. Mara, a short, slim and black rich man is a retired army officer who born on 1934 in Kyawaza village during the brishis colonial rule in Tanzaland.

He is a very known rich pastoralist with over one thousand cows, four thousand goats and thousands of sheep, let alone birds which are as many as hard to count.

Mr. Mara is two times more notable for his polygamous beliefs and Life. As for a known random number, he has married up to fifty two wives, he is approximately to have more than one hundred known children and more than two hundred known grandchildren and still marries and reproducing kids to date.

As other Kurya tribesmen, Mr. Mara believes that having a large number of wives is a pride of a kurya man also having great number of male children is termed as manpower and a capital when having lots daughters especially when a father or a male guardian receive their bride prices.

A Heartbreaking Tale

It was a night of 1976 only three days to new year eve. Anna, a 17 year old young Kurya village girl who was a fourth wife of Mr.Mara gave birth to a beautiful baby boy who was named Jean afterwards.

The night was so beautiful to both young parents because having a child in Kurya tribe is an indicator of respect, growing up and bravery and what really mattered the most, the child was actually a baby boy with the exact likenesses of Mr. Mara himself because having the likeness of a father to some people means alot. Everyone in the village and family envied Mr. Mara because he is adding much more manpower into his household.

Mr. Mara would eventually tell everyone about these exciting news and anyone would see him smile and exciting even from afar.

Though everyone seemed to be happy about Anna giving birth to a son, the other wives of Mr. Mara were really upset about the news because they thought that Anna would get some more favors over them because she was the youngest and fine wife of Mr. Mara's wives additionally, she now has given Mr. Mara a beautiful son but neither Mr.Mara nor Anna gave attention to hatred brought by other wives of Mr.Mara.

Per Kurya traditions, Anna was given gifts and lots of cows, goats and sheeps as rewards because Kurya is a pastoral tribe and this was the only happiest moment of Anna's life anyone could ever remember.

****

Anna, a girl from a neighborhood town was a a light skinned african younglady with a figured body and straight thick black hair, blessed by beauty that would make any man fall for her because of her cuteness. Alot of people would be heard calling her an angel sometimes.

Despite being one of the hottest ladies more than almost any lady in Kyawaza village, Anna was still an illiterate property that any man with money would buy her in the name of marriage.

Her luck did not turn out well because lastly, Anna the most beautiful village girl was bought by naught Mr. Mara.

Anna started her marriage life as a fourth wife of Mr. Mara whom she only gave birth to only one child in her lifetime until her sudden death occured lived her life to yhe happiest until she was sold to a careless man who was blinded by local customs and would never think of a well-being of female human over himself.

After giving birth to Jean, Anna was a beloved wife of Mr. Mara though he loved his other wives as well but not as much as he loved Anna at that time.

The love of Mr. Mara for Anna and her child Jean was unbearable to his other three wives at a time, to the extent that they would do anything for Mr. Mara and Anna get into conflicts or even get anna divorced.

Anna came for love but she was now in a critical smooth war with her fellow wives. She was still young to even start arguments to an elder sister but now she was forced to have a proper serious battle.

Anna was helpless indeed because she was still young,

immature and still needed a guide to get used to marriage life but those weak points of hers gave power to her fellow wives get into her nerves and lastly won over her.

At a time she was accused of things she have never even dreamed of doing, she was accused of cheating, stealing and sometimes laziness. Other wives of Mr. Mara could not stand her outside beauty and love she got from their husband so, making her look bad inside was their own remained option.

Repeated beatings and torture from her husband, Mr. Mara kept her on the bed for too long bleeding and untreated at the same time having a child to breastfeed .

Lastly the life of a young, beautiful and kind Anna ended miserably because of hatred from fellow wives also the beatings and torture from her husband.

Jean was 2 months old at the time when her mother passed away, what a sad life would be for the kid.

For some years Jean would try to tolerate all kinds of torments he would get from his step mothers and step siblings but in a real sense, he could never win that battle.

He had done a lot of miserable work at such a young age, he once made charcoal and sold them, a 12 years old Jean, making charcoal from a growing tree, means he would cut a couple of big trees, prepare a furnance to burn them to charcoal all by himself, parking the charcoal and all by

t3himself take them to nearby village's rich individuals to sell them and once he got the cents, his tep guardians would snatch all of them telling him that if they ever charged him for food he has been eating all the days.

Jean to shift to his crippled uncle called Mnik who was living in a nearby more developed village at a place where he met Fauna and his younger brother Carl.

Mnik was abrother in law to Mr. Mara also a blood big brother of Anna, Jean's birth mother who had died only two months after she gave birth to Jean.

Mnik lived far from Mr. Mara's village because he was atleast educated and would never allow his children to be swallowed with his tribe's legacies and illiteracy, that's why Mnik's children had reached a certain level of education compared to Kyawaza's residents.

Mnik was known for his aggressive behaviours though he was crippled on both legs, he was also famous for his local medicines that people accused him to a witch and later on he was badly burned inside his house because people thought that he has been bewitching them, and that was a sad ending of Mnik, Jean's uncle who raised him up as his own son.

Jean seems to be forgetting about his wife and two kids, what will Aggie do?

Intelligent Kid Comes

A certain wise person said, "the best place to hide is your enemy's tent," Jean, a two months old infant was already in enemies hands. He was really innocent and he would do nothing to defend himself even when attacked.

Jean was raised and breastfed to one of Mr. Mara's wives who made his mother's killing possible.

Jean had to get a parent for his survival, he was at the age when he needed his mother's milk the most but he had nowhere to breastfeed.

Mr. Mara wanted this child to survive no matter what, he would never bear to stand again if this kid had died because at a time he felt too much guilty for his beloved wife's death and would never his son to die.

Mr. Mara had to act like a real father he thought about that for a while and finnaly got an answer. He forcefully found a mother among his wives who recently had bornt a son called Toma (Chale's younger brother), she was called Mama Chale, whom she was forced to breastfeed and raise Jean because she was among the great reasons for Mr. Mara get into conflicts and at last killed his beloved wife, Anna. At that time, little Toma was a few days old, so Mama Chale had to live like she gave birth to twin brothers, who occasionally grew together and loved one another as real brothers and that was Jean's lucky charm.

****

As a young kid, Jean had to endure all of the torture he would get from his step mothers, elder step brothers and sisters. Luckily, Jean was so much loved by his father Mr. Mara who would eventually praise him when he had achieved something, raised him up when he fell and would do anything to help his little boy when in need, all because he was a son to his most beloved wife, Anne as per people's stories but I think he would do all those because he felt guilt for whatever the mistakes he had done to Jean and his mother, that was some kind of seeking forgiveness or easy the burden he was carrying on his head.

As years passed by, Jean grew up and at the age of six, he was sent to school that was recently opened in Kyawaza in favour of his father who would never give priority to schooling and education because he had the same beliefs as the local men of his tribes that a real man should have a large number of cows, wives, children and a big piece of land.

Jean never dissapointed his father, he was indeed a genius kid of all of of his brothers and sisters, he would often be the the first in his class and he would get presents for his studies excels. He later on joined Madara secondary school, a secondary school found on a nearby village he went on studying but dropped out because he did not receive further educational support from Mr. Mara who was his only support.

Mr. Mara would not support him anymore because, his polygamous behavior gave him lots of children to care too and at this time he had more than twenty wives and fifty children to feed, give shelter and provide other required expenses as a father.

Not only Jean but other children who were at school had

to drop out because none would sponsor them anymore.
As time paseed by Mr. Mara could not afford raising all the children and giving them all the required needs, all he had to do was introducing a new strict rule that, since he would never dare sending his daughters to school, he would accept bride prices from any village man whether a boy, man or an old man who wished to pay for his daughter and would accept the offer to even twelve years old daughter, and so and anyone who dared impregnate his daughter would marry and pay the higher prices even if the force was required. As for the boys, they were all needed to drop out of school since no one was going to pay their school fees also if anyone had reached fifteen years and older should look for a place to go and start his life but he would give favour to stay for any of his sons if a son would get a job and being something at home and that was done so to Jean.
Since Jean was a brilliant kid both at home and school and was on his father's favour, even after he had dropped out of school because of lack of financial support, Mr. Mara got him a job to one of germans' mineral transporting company he had connections with since his old days as a soldier and Jean was recruited as a security watchman.
Jean's brilliance and hardworking was seen by his bosses (the germans) and he was loved much more than the other employers and eventually he was promoted to be the chief head security to that Germany company. It reached a time when the germans had finished their contracts and it was their time to ho back home but, since they loved Jean's spirit of working they offered this village boy a chance to go with them in Germany promising him a pay raise, good life and additional privileges. Jeans was so happy because

among all those who were sweating to work with the germans he was the only chosen one to go with them! He had to go, he eventually would never let this to slip from his hands, he had to grab it tightly. He went on giving Mr. Mara these exciting news and was seeking for his permission from his family to try his lucky abroad.

At that time Jean had already married miss Aggie (next chapter) and had already had two sons with her so Mr. Mara would never hesitate to say a big no to Jean and if he eagerly wanted that permission he was given an option and that was to pack up and take his family with him to Germany. Eventually the germany didn't want Jean's family they only needed Jean's manpower and brilliance so they could never say yes to Jean's family. Only one option for Jean had remained and that was to remain in Kyawaza and even if he wanted to snitch away with the germans he could never succeed because an official approval from his father and village leaders (who were both his father, Mr. Mara) were needed. He had to accept the defeat this time round.

From that moment on Jean hated his family so much and had seen a family as a burden to him.

Unintentionally Marriage

Despite Jean being an intelligent young lad, he was born and raised into an illiterate village so he had adopted and lived the same lifestyle as the rest of the village boys of his age. When he reached 19 years old Jean had to marry and start his own life though he was still living at his father's place.

Marrying at such a young age in villages is normal and a sign of maturity to boys.

Jean got himself a young fine lady called Aggie, one of the older daughters of Roba, Mr. Mara's neighbor.

Aggie was the second daughter of elder Roba Nyanke, she was a white-skinned, short lovely girl, she had a little structure that would one think that she was still a young girl but infact she was a matured young lady.

Jean never loved or wanted to marry aggie, he truly loved Aggie's young sister, Tinde, who looked much more sexy due to her fine built body structure compared to Aggie who was a little bit slim and little. Tinde never loved Jean, and Jean never loved Aggie, while aggie really loved Jean and wished he would be married to him.

Aggie would do anything to make Jean fall for her and since Jean was assisting Aggie on writing and reading extra studies at home, it was easy for Jean to fall for her traps and lastly they found their marriage unavoidable.

Aggie was already proposed and her pride price was

already paid at a time she was dating Jeans and a night before marriage, she escaped to Jean's hut without tellinga nyone except her older sister who understood her feelings for Jean. So, Jean had to forcefully marry her if it will come to be known that she was in her hut the night of her marriage, at this level Aggie was much more wiser than Jean because, per her plot, she would easily convince people (especiall her parents) that Jean aided her as he helped her run away from a man who was about to marry her and since she well knew the conclusion that it will be a marriage of these two, she was winning over him and she thought he would be forever hers afterwards.
How would Mr. Roba solve this puzzle?
After a long, long night looking for their daughter without finding her, they decided to give up on her. But, to keep his family's dignity, all Mr. Roba had to do was giving the bridegroom Aggie's younger sister, Tinde (Jean's crush) in Aggie's place who was younger, much more beautiful and still a virgin at a time, based on all those, her bride price was approximately to be much more higher than Aggie's. That means Mr. Roba had an investment on losses and he would never accept that shit. Somebody had to pay for this because no one would ever imagine that Aggie would plot this all by herself without getting help from outside.
The World is a small place for a word of mouth, that's what happened. Early on the next day, the news of Aggie running away from her wedding was all over the village and some of Jean's friends had seen her entering Jean's hut, so Jean was caught red handed in broad daylight and he had entered Aggie's traps very easily (some sources with unproven facts suggested that, it is true Jean had all impacts on Aggie's plotting, he and her elder sister knew all

that was going on and he promised to marry her in case she succeeded on running away from her bridegroom but I will go with this known and well told source).

Aggie's running away had a meaning that Jean was a mastermind behind all this running, and what was next then? Jean had to pay for all the mess he caused, and eventually in such a big occasion Mr. Mara would never have been left behind because Jean was never able to pay for anything, imagine paying back all the bride price the family had lost, and in Kurya tribes, the bride prices are not as cheap as in other communities, one had to pay dozens of cows, goats and couple of other requirements to take a girl or bride (some even find themselves in a lifetime debts if they fail to pay in one go).

Mr. Mara would never deny paying for all the mess his son had caused, starting with fine, and taking in Aggie as her daughter in law by paying her bride price instead of Jean who was too poor to pay that was much more higher that what would be paid if she was proposed directly from her parents. Mr. Mara had to do this in order to keep his glorious family's dignity that he has planted and watered for so many years.

The marriage between Jean who was nineteen at a time and Aggie who was sixteen at a time is a good example of an early marriage, the type of marriages that do not last longer because of immaturity of both partners.

Without having courtship or even loving one another, they made it into marrying and starting a family.

In real sense, Agness was a talkative short tempered lady when angry also the same goes to Jean who was an aggressive short tempered lad when angry, that means only a small matter would get them freak out because of their temper and they would find themselves in a real fight vecause Jean's only quick way of solving any problem was a fight, and Aggie's way of dealing with matters was lamenting, crying, talking loudly and blaming.

As other married couples, Jean and Aggie as young teenagers had a fine start and would enjoy the family life fully and would never think if someday they will part ways in the worst type of way.

Will Jean and Aggie enjoy their marriage life? Will Aggie's family accept and love fully Jean as their newly son in law?

The Psychopath

On 1997, Jean and Aggie held their marriage locally with alot of pressure from both parents and that day marked the starting of their marriage life which they though to be as sweet as their golden dating days but the never realized that, their marriage was an outcome of their hurry, sex affection, teenage pressures and parents decisions but love, respect or understanding to one onother never played any role in between their marriage.

The first year of their marriage really flew well and on April 16th, 1999 they had their first son, I, Mara Jose Mara 'Joe' who became the eldest grandchild of Mr. Mara.

I know it is hard to understand how did I, or simply Joe became the elderst grandchild of Mr. Mara when the other wives of Mr. Mara had children too who actually would have older children at a time Joe was born. Yes, it is correct that Mr. Mara had other grandchildren from other wives who were much older compared to little Joe but, sadly they were both females or simply girls.

let me tell you a little secret, in many of Tanzaland's tribes including my tribe, the Kurya tribe never count the daughters as the rightful full family members, that they can never inherent anything from family's fortune, they can never make any accepted decision in family matters, they can never choose anything for themselves and will never use a father's name after they are married, so that is how

Joe got all the rights to be the eldest grandchild of Mr. Mara though he was never the first child to be born from Mara's children.

Me or simply Joe, was a dark black skinned, short, and a fat kid who was a mixture of a mother and father. He did not resemble just one side but all the two sides from grandfathers and grandmothers to both parents, he never took sides from his likenesses to his ways of living.

Jean was still living with his family of three and working as a recruit in Kyawaza village and on 2001two years later, Jean and Aggie were blessed to have another child whom they called Frankie, a fat white-coloured child with a huge body structure since his birth, gladly he was again the second eldest grandchild of Mr. Mara.

Frankie was born between a controversial period where Jean and Aggie were in grave conflicts, that drove Aggie curse Frankie who was still an infant in her stomach and she swore that, sge would rather kill jim before birth that giving birth to him all because of his father and she was sometimes heard saying that she was indeed tired of marriage life and wished to be all alone.

Though Aggie was a short tempered lady, she really loved Jean that it was really hard for her to allow any other village girl vome near him.

One of the behaviors Aggie never noticed grom Jena was that, Jean was actually a polygamist in nature and would never be satisfied dating or sleeping over with only one woman throughout, so he was indeed cheating on Aggie and Aggie would eventually get in touch with these hurting news or even eye witnessing and whenever she dared speaking or lamenting anything about them, she could end up covered by blood from her own wounds she got from

Jean's cruelly type of beating and she was sometimes treated as a harlot or a prostitute but in reality, she was a rightful and known wife of Jean Mara

Since the marriage between Jean and Aggie was never a both-sides love, it was actually predicted to break someday anyways, and it was moving to it's peak and this was the right right time it all started.

Jean loved Fauna, his niece one of uncle Mnik's daughters whom they had secretly started a secret relationship since the old days they were both living under Mr. Mnik's house. Another secret is that, per one of marriage Jewish cultures, it is very normal for a man to marry his auntie's or uncle's daughter(as Bible's Isaac married uncle Raban's daughters Leah and Rachel), they consider them as not having a closely kinship or relationship to the extent that they can not marryone another. As Kurya ancestors always said that Kurya people might be the descendants of Jews one could simply agree based on this marriage reason. In Kurya tribe a man is regally allowed to marry his niece if he happen to love her or if his parents choose her for him (not only in Kurya tribe but many more other known tribes are known to be practising this kind of culture, even I myself do not think if it is too bad).

Jean came with a reason that he wanted to find new life out of Kyawaza village and new life challenges far away from Mr. Mara's territory, so he shifted to a nearby region and a large city called Manza Town but, tbough he might as well went for the reasons he mentioned but as far as we know he actually followed Fauna who was working in Manza Town as a magazine saleswoman to be with her and enjoy their so called love, also as a youth who never thought if a man can marry at any age not a must at his age (he got this experience a time he once visited Manza Town), he wanted to run way from his family to be the same as town men, that was the beginning of Jean and Aggie's conflicts.

Jean started working as a day worker to house builders where he learned basics to building a house and balancing all the building requirements to get the quality house but he had no experience to start that job as a builder because no one trusted him at the moment with less experience so, he decided to keep on learning but he got a job that he went for and left behind all the construction classes he has been taking recently and maybe if that job did not interfere in between, Jean would be a house builder to date.

How was Aggie and the kids at the village?

A Root of All Evils

Days passed by, months vanished and Jean was now too deep into Fauna's love that he completely forgot his family at home and was even ready to dump them to start a fresh life with Fauna.

Why was Jean so deep in love with Fauna? Was she beautiful more than Aggie?

****

Fauna had a dark-lighted skin, a well figured body, kind, and a huster who escaped village customs and was now an independent woman from local stupid beliefs, I would hear Jean (My father) calling her a back beauty angel, she indeed was beautiful per his view.

Aggie who was left behind with two sons, Joe and Frankie tried to reach Jean (his husband) without a success because Jean cut all the possible means of communications between them he really did not want his family again and would think of them as a burden to him.

Jean was severally reminded of his family in the village and was told to send some money to his wife for the family but he sometimes was dodging his responsibilities.

Aggie was still living in Jean's hut that he built for his family back in Kyawaza village. Jean could never afford to care for Jean's children alm by herself because she was only a housewife and she had no education that would give her an opportunity to feed the kids, Joe who was two years at a time and Frankie who was only a seven months old kid at that time. Jean left his family in between a hatred big clan because a large number of Mr. Mara's family never loved Jean's mother thus transfer that hatred to Jean and his family. so, leaving a helpless Aggie and the kids in the village was a real insult to someone's daughter, at that time Jean would never care because he was in love with someone else and he never loved Aggie or the children either.

Aggie decided to talk to his father in law, Mr. Mara about his son's behavior of dumping them without sending anything and would never care on how they survive and also since love is like a cough and would never hide whenever someone got it, Agness received a lot of people laments of Jean dating Fauna while leaving her and his family behind, so that was also among the head topics in that short meeting.

Though Mr. Mara was very hard to reach and talk with because he was now a very busy man due to his crowded and still growing family with more than a hundred family members. Agness had that chance easily because Mr. Mara closely cared about Jean's affairs, and after hearing all of his son's blames he reached him through a village phone which were scarce at that time adding that the village he was in was Kyawaza. Due to kids bad living conditions and kids poor healthcare, Mr. Mara urgently called Jean to the village so as to witness what was really happening to his family and to answer all the accusation Agness filed to his father also to give a proper conclusion on how he was going to handle the situation.

****

Jean arrived in the village few days later eagerly to hear

whatever he was called for, after a warm welcome and a rest, Mr. Mara and other family leaders were called to hear out Jean's case and give out their opinions concerning Jean and his family. After an anrgument that lasted too long, at last they came into a conclusion that Jean should go wherever he is going with his family and should never again leave them alone whether he wanted or doesn't want. Though unwillingly, Jean headed back to Manza Town to make preparations for his family to arrive and settle with him, who really arrived few days after.

The life of Agness started in a town she has never been, with a husband she was never loved, with kids that nobody wanted and with a strong enemy (Fauna) she has never battled.

The life in Manza Town was neither good to Agness, the kids , Fauna nor because everyone was battling his or her own stressful moments.

The two kids were sad because they never had a peaceful life as in the village because their parents would ways fight ans sometimes they were added to a fight they don't even know what it is all about, looking at Frankie only a seven months old baby blamed for the mistake he would never do at a time could not even walk all by himself.

Fauna was not happy because she no longer felt secure because her lover's wife was ther and she would no longer get daily chances of enjoying Jean's love also since Aggie knew all that was goinv on between her and her husband, Fauna would not rest assured because though Aggie has a small figure, she was not an easy opponent to deal with.

Aggie was never happy because she was sometimes accused, insulted and beaten badly in a shameful manner, sometimes infront of people of mistakes she never did, all that she was never wanted, loved or required and she knew all these.

Jean was never happy because he was the source of all the problems and these priblems would eventually bounce back to his own face, he was really embarrassed by all the stupidity he has done but he would go on living in mistakes he created and try covering them but not solving or puting an end to them. He would never feel at ease because he was no longer free to roam about and enjoy the love of lover of his life becaues of Aggie and her kids, secondly he repeatedly found himself into fight with Aggie who was a short tempered individual as he was, he ended up beating her up badly and use alot of costs sending her to hospital.

The biggest reason of all reasons is that, Jean was now living with a people he never wanted into his life. Imagine, forever living with a perosn you never love under the same roof, that was really disgusting to him living together with kids and a wife while he had a youth life to take care of.

Dumped

Even though Aggie or Jean were both happy living with one another, that would never be an obstacle for them to have another kid.

Only two months later Aggie was pregnant and was expecting another third child the thing that Jean never wanted to hear.

Aggie's pregnancy was never accepted by Jean, he kept believing that; somehow, Aggie had cheated him and slept with another man who is a real father to that unborn kid and swore that he would never accept that kid, and even sometimes, Aggie was beaten badly forcing her to tell him and others that the kid was never his.

****

The moment Aggie felt like he had Jean's pregnancy, Jean was already shifted to Karage, a nearby region to work as a magazine salesman, a business he and Fauna have been doing in Manza Town.

At a time Jean shifted shifted to Karage, Aggie had to stay much longer in Manza Town but they later on were required to return to the village (Kyawaza) because Jean was never there to take care of them and he would promise to take rhem with him once he has settled in Karage, the promise rather seemed to be a fake one because Jean wanted a space, he wanted to be far from Aggie and his family and he had one! What would he wish

to have again? Would Aggie expect to be called to Karage to be with Jean? Hell no!!
Surprisingly, not only Agness but also Fauna felt like she was pregnancy to Jean's child, the secret they were hiding was finally coming to it's exposure. That was really a controversial moment for Jean and would be for anyone whobwould be in that situation, rember that Jean and Fauna has been dating secretly and suddenly they weee expecting a child without any family leader knowing that, though elders would hear the rumors concerning Jean and Fauna, they would consider them as only speculations since Jean and Fauna would deny those accusations.
Jean started convincing Fauna concerning abortion and he won over her, he came with reasons that he was already a married man and his uncle (Fauna's father, Mnik) would never understand him. Fauna had to understand because he loved Jean without having a second thoughts that, even Aggie really loved Jean but he was certainly dumped together with two kids that the same would happen to him.
After all these controversies, Jean managed to settle down and had started a new life in a small town of Bimulo district, one of five districts of Karage region though the polygamous blood flowing inside of him could never let go of him, he forgot all about Aggie, Children and Fauna after he started loving his friend's girlfriend that put him into another life-threatening Controversy.

****

Aggie left Manza Town and headed back to the village full of confidence that Jean was there preparing a home sweet home far, far away from the village for himself and her family but only Jean knew what he was doing in Bimulo, he would only think and taln of his family when he was reminded and as time went on, he found that he gave very much attention to his current life and would rest assured because he never heard of his child's death, that meant to him that they were both fine.

Aggie waited very long to the extent that she could not torelate it anymore, she felt cheated, dumped, thrown aside and left behind to care for the family all by herself because whenever she talked to Jean about family reunion, Jean would never give a straight-forward proper answer, he always hinted about life difficulties and starting a new home was never easy as he thought and that Bimulo's life was too much expensive for him to have and handle a family so he always insisted her to keep on waiting though the truth was that, Jean had started earning and making some money and Bimulo's life was never as difficult as he elaborated it. He only never wanted Aggie and his kids.

After Aggie had realized that he was treated as a dumpster, he made a very big desion that changed lives of herself, her children and Jean's. Aggie was still young and beautiful at that time, she would never miss someone to marry her and so, she decided to part ways with Jean but in a very strict and cruelest way. Aggie decided to dump the two kids (Joe and Frankie) as well leaving a real heartbreaking message that to her children were like faeces she would eventually defecate any amount when she is filled, that sentence has always rolled in between the two kids name up to date, it is the same sentence that hinder them to forgive their mother until today.

A father abandoned the wife and kids without providing them with anything, without any security when they are attacked, without showing love whenever they needed it yhe kost, he was never there the time they needed him the most and sometimes a mother gets angry and too abandon the kids without anyone to wash them when they are dirty, none to give them medicine when they are sick, none to feed them when they are hungry and no one to defend them whenever thay are bullied. These parents (Jean and Aggie) simply never cared if the kids would live or even die, all they cared about was their happiness and feelings.

Joe was two years old and Frankie was only a nine months old kid at the time when a mother decided to dump them too as their father had done few months ago. In between the house of hatred, the house of Mr. Mar where no one cares about somebody's child let alone Jean's children, the two kids who could not even run proper were left to survive, atleast for Joe, he was abit grown-up but, Frankie was only nine months old, that was so sad and devastating. Will Joe and Frankie survive? Will Aggie return for his children? How will Jean react after hearing this sad news?

A Dim Survival

It was really hard for the two kids to survive in such a bad condition, with no anyone to take care of them or look after them, they were begging food to other familie whenever they saw them eating, these two kids were actually treated as outcasts, they were given the leftover foods as dogs, the were never allowed to eat on the same table with anyone because they were simply dirty, only rainfall was a blessing to them because, as it rained, they would get the chance to atleast cleanse their bodies though they would shiver after that and since no one was there to give them any coat or jacket, the only solution to them was entering inside their parents' hut and cry until they both fall asleep. Mr. Mara was now a real busy many because of his then big family, he would not go on each hut to check if everybody was alright unless a report has reached him, thay means he knew nothing of Jean's kids, Joe and a nine months onld Frankie.

Things went on for weeks and now months, until one good samaritan (I can not well explain about this person because I never got to know the exact person i.e gender, likeness, age, or even relationship) found two starving and isolated kids in the worst condition who needed quick help if they were to survive any longer. A good samaritan did everything he or she could do to help the kids.

****

Jean never bothered about Aggie or village life because he knew his family would eventually survive because he handed them over his father's family care and thought that; if he managed to survive in such a condition without any siblings or mother, then, who are they to fail surviving on the same family with the same people and same hatred? Jean had started being very selfish and a little bit of a wicked man, forgetting all he has been through and should never repeat the same to his kids. One's lucky and fate is already sealed on forehead before he or she is born. Who was Jean to think that the family would actually survive if he too survived the same conditions?

Fauna had left resigned from her job as a magazine salesman to live with Jean in Bimulo who was also a magazine agent and salesman in Bimulo, simply because she too loved him and would do these simple sacrifice to be with Jean who loved her too.

The fact that Fauna was living together with Jean would make them both feel like they are now a newly couple in honeymoon hence, family would eventually be forgotten.

When the news concerning Joe and Frankie had reached Jean, he was very much confused and felt too much regrets because he thought on how silly he had became to leave the kids behind and enjoy all by himself, he once never wanted them because they were hindrances to his golden chances like a chance he missed of flying abroad to Germany.

****

Jean quickly arranged to leave for his abandoned kids in Kyawaza village because he has heard that Aggie no longer want either marriage or the kids anymore and they were left alone inside an old hut he built couple of years back.

He and Fauna had to leave together but he had to leave Fauna in Manza Town to simply reduce unwanted noise pollution in Kyawaza because the moment they had seen Fauna they wouls accuse her of breaking Jean's marriage also at that time, Jean had not officially taken in Fauna as his regal wife.

He could never imagine how cruel was Aggie until the day he saw the kids and witnessed whatever he was given as stories.

The moment he saw them(the kids), the first and possible thing he could do was crying loudly he could never believed to see his kids in such a bad condition. He found Joe in between cows legs stuck in their accumulated faeces where he went to try fetching milk for himself and frankie because he always sees women and grown-ups going in there and caming out with gallons full of milk so, he though he would get some milk in there, he was really hungry, that was his second day since he and frankie had their last little meal, which was eventually a leftoverfoods. How could they do if not trying to look for food all by themselves. When Jeanhad a side to side looking aside he saw his little boy, Frankie stuck too on entrance to cows' shed and would not move even one single step forward what a risky game this two kids were playing because if cows had to have a little movement they would both be dead even before Jean was there.

Jean quickly took his kids out of cows' shits, bathed them and quickly rushed to Madarak, a small nearby trading center where he sent them to a salon to have a shave because their hair were dirty, with shabby looks and had grown long to the extent that it was difficult for someone to differentiate the two kids with two little human-like monkeys (joking), he bought them new pairs of clothes and new sandals to wear.

From that moment on, neither Joe nor Fra kie have ever returned to the village because Jean found a guest room in Madarak for himself and the kids for that day and very early on the next morning he took his kids to leave for Bimulo to live together with them.

Manza Town is found somewhere between Kyawaza and Bimulo so one had to take a day rest or so if he wanted to reach Bimulo because there's no a direct bus from Kyawaza to Bimulo even up to date. In Manza Town, Fauna was waiting for Jean and the kids to head back to Bimulo together.

Jean had to follow all the possible protocols and took in Fauna as his wife because he needed someone to take care of the kids and since he had someone he really loved and that's how Fauna became Joe and Frankie's mother.

New Life, New Beginning

Jean and Fauna had started a family as new parents as 'Mama Mara' and 'Baba Mara' (Mara is another name for Joe) and since no one at Bimulo knew thair actual backgrounds, people would think Joe and Frankie were their sons left on their old hometown, without knowing that Fauna was only a step mother to the kids.

Fauna had her first son with Jean only few months after they had settled down while Joe and Frankie were still growing up as nice and beautiful kids.

The first son of Jean and Fauna was Kevl who just died only a few months later but they had another child five years later on.

****

Joe as a little kid was a fat, short, and black kid but changed gradually at a time as he was growing up, Frankie was the same as he was a kid, a white kid who had quick growth the fact that made people have difficulties in identifying who was the elder son of Mama and Baba Mara between Joe and Frankie. All in all, life was going as smooth as water flowing from mouth passing through esophagus to the stomach all because Jean was now a grown-up man who would easily identify which was right and what really mattered is that, fauna had accepted whole-heartedly raising Jean's sons as their new mother.

As time flew by, Fauna was again pregnant for the second

child (her firstborn child Kevl, had just died few months after he was born) and in the middle of 2004 he had a son and named him Cyfford, from that moment on, Fauna had to live like a real mother not only to Cyfford but to both three children.

On the same year 2004, little Joe who was now five, had to start attending to an elementary school where he had to learned reading and and writing before joining a primary school, he was supposed to attend an elementary school for two years as ordinary students do and because of his small figure, his parents would not think twice on adding him another year at school. But Joe surprised everyone because he was way better smarter than any of the pupils at his level, he would read and write so well like a standard two pupil and that was his direct ticket to fly to standard one having studied one full year as an elementary pupil.

Frankie was too young to start attending to school, all time long he would stay at home with baby Cyfford and playing baby games with other street children of his level. Two years later on 2005, he joined the same elementary school as Joe's.

All that time Jean was working as a newspapers salesman and Fauna would start frying and selling fish, a business that would keep the family going.

Jean would not just sit idle selling newspapers and magazines at his kiosk, he had started taking online studies from a certain abroad college because he wanted to make a big different of him from an illiterate person.

Jean and Fauna were both the baptized Seventh Day Adventists or simply SDAs, that means Joe, Frankie and Cyfford would grow up in a religious environments, what a nice foundation these two parents were building to their children. Joe went on to become a choir member only at the age of 8 at a time where the youngest choir member in their church was oly 21 years old, the great courage of little Joe opened eyes of alot of SDA parents and encouraged their children that they could serve Almight God eveb starting from a very young age like Joe (the last time I visited few of Bimulo's SDA churches, I would see alot of young boys and girls singing and praising loudly, wearing beautiful choir uniforms as the choir members), infact, Joe was the first to do that at Bimulo, all thanks to Fauna and Jean's foundation.

Jean had loved money since ages but it was on this point that he eagerly wanted to have it like hell, apart from normal struggles, he had started attending to witch doctors looking for wealthy forgetting that he was a good christian and his family needed his lead to have a well planned lives on the future.

If a person had known Jean since he was a little child, he would not bother wondering on how Jean Prefers money to anything else. Jean has always lived on revenge and he had kept his vengeance for years but he was the only child from his deceased mother, to others he looked almost like an outcast and a powerless child, the only solution to keep all these under control was looking for power wherever it was hiding after he had known that money is power itself. He would look money anywhere with all his strength, with all his power and with all his energy.

Jean once reached a stage where he was willing to sacrifice his firstborn child, Joe for money. He was told to sacrifice his own firstborn fresh with a promise of getting millions of united states dollars inside a locker he was given, he agreed (per witnesses) but luckily was with Joe because those people acted to be witch doctors were actually scammed and he was canned very interestingly but, if they were actual witch doctors, you could never get someone to give you this beautiful story book today.

On this moment on, Jean was making great connections with alot of people because he was the only newspapers salesman in the whole district and everybody would come frim all parts of the town to get newspapers, hemanaged to get rich people because since newspapers were the only quick source of quick news right after radios at that time, they would make special orders that their newspapers should be kept aside for them before thay are finished due to people's scrambling.

These connections made him reach the most important people on his life including Mr. Mikila and Yusup who both played a great role on his futureife achievements.

Road to Prosperity

Jean came to the sweetest stage of his life, a poor and abandoned village boy was now the richest man of the whole Bimulo district. How did he manage to achieve that? Since ages, on his growth stages, Jean has never been lazy or a fool, despite all of his other problems, Jean was among the smartest and intelligent people I have ever seen. He would be the first to get easy answers to problems, he would never let anything go with excuses of failure, failure was never welcomed into his life.

****

One rich old engineer whom I only knew by a single name Mikila, who was a big fan of newspapers, found himself a great friend of Jean who was the only newspapers agent at Bimulo and since mobile phones were scarce at that time in Tanzaland not only Bimulo, newspapers and magazines were at the peak of their selling business.

Through their friendship and stories Mikala came to learn that Jean was among the genius poor people at Bimulo and he would never allow that asset to slip eventually all he needed was use Jean's brain for his own success.

Jean had started working in Mikila's construction company as a deputy proffesional engeneer though he never had any proffesional certificates in engineering, he was much more better than any worker in his company since Jean would speak and write english fluently even more than Mikila himself, (you could only find a few number of people at that time speaking english at Jean's level), he would help the company on writing, understanding and signing the contracts. Secondly, Jean was a mathematics genius who had approximately an accuracy of about 89 percent. Third, Jean had learned construction methods, important basics and procedures way back when he was a day worker in Manza Town, so his basics would make him fit for a construction company for that reason.

Jean was very happy because he was a man of living his ego and living his job of selling tge newspapers was a great news for him because he thought maybe that job underrated him, he needed a new and proffesional job and here he was.

Jean went on working at Mikila's construction company for more than two years. I barely remember, he once worked for nine months without getting even a week break but the whole family had to understand him because he was not trying to abandon them as before, he was now trying harder to give them a better life.

God saw this young man who was struggling to make his life better and blessed him, a poor village boy was now capable of holding his own bundles of notes. The family was very happy and he would show and explain to them all the blessings God has shown and given him.

Not only Jean, Mikila's crew including Mr. Mikila himself was happy because they got all the best they hoped from Jean and it was Jean's turn to part way with Mikila's construction company and start his own preferred business but Jean chose to keep on working on construction companies and had wished to have his own construction company one day.

Jean joined hands with Chale and Toma (these were the sons of Mama Chale, Mr. Mara's wife who raised Jean right after his mother's dmsudden death) and together they formed a construction company and named it after their great grandfather's name and Chale would become it's first Managing director because he was the eldest of all three brothers and was a bit more than all financially.

Nyama General Promotion and Supplies LTD or simply 'NGPS' was the name these three brothers had thought and given their newly construction company and the work started.

NGPS started pretty cool but since money doesn't know relatives, they never took long before they would start fighting over shares, leadership, and bias among themselves, they could no longer agree or love one another or stay together any more the fact that caused anemity among themselves and their families to date.

Toma was an intermediate man and would never bother taking any side and not hated him, the real problem was between Jean and Chale. Jean woukd think Chale was treating him as an outcast since he had no mother and would not share with him equally for whatever they were earning and Chale would think Jean was pretending to be much more smarter than any of them and would want control everything so, money won over them.

NGPS never died but it was shaken somehow and finally, the brothers had to agree on working separately though they had to be under one company.

That agreement gave Jean a chance to shine over his brothers because he lived on a city (Bimulo) where they needed him the most, it was still a small and developing town at that time means alot of construction was needed in

the city.
Only few years later, Jean had bought his first Land Cruiser 4WD left handed car not only that, he had started the construction to his own mansion in Ng'ambo village in Bimulo. Life was never hard again for Jean, Fauna and their three kids, Joe, Frankie and Cyfford.
A moment later this beautiful family had moved to their new and big house in Ng'ambo village, only one and a half kilometers from Bimulo Town. Even though their house wasn't completely finished in terms of floor, painting or roof, they had no any other choice but to hop in because they were eagerly moving to their own legal home and actually they were both tired of rent houses.
Jean returned to work and sometimes later he happened to hit a bingo for a one moment, that was when he got a job from one chinese company where he would help them in constructing small road-slabs and was paid handsomely, he found that he was earning ten times than how he was earning before.
He hit a second bingo when he got a job on a nearby district to supply water throughout a village, a work that made him make his own construction company apart from NGPS because he never wanted something called sharing, he had to be a bit 'selfish' too.
Later on, Jean would go and own dozens of cars both luxury and working cars, he owned a couple of mansions in Bimulo and had invested alot without forgetting on the pieces of lands he owned.

Polygamous Hell

Few of Jean's great weaknesses were women and sex, As I said before, Jean would never ever stay put with only one woman at home and get satisfied with her. He would eventually wish to have every woman who would get across his way.

The first days of his first marriage (with Aggie) he would eventually wish to be with Fauna, her cousin means he was cheating Aggie at that time, I pity Fauna because he would not think about allowing a cheating married man to marry and take her in.

Few days after Jean got the one he tbought that he was in love with (Fauna), he would eventually cheat her again by seducing his friends' wives, cases that would put him into very very dangerous situations, reaching the stage that he had received a couple of death threats and as far as I can recall, he once was imprisoned for only a few days because of his friend's wife.

After tasting jail's heat, he would not go after married women again, he was looking for those who will not give him more troubles and he lastly he would go after his own workers. At times he was still working at a magazine kiosk, he had slept with his own secretary, Fauna had torelated Jean's behavior and he would insist him on remembering that he has family, anything wrong he will be doing will not not only let him down, but he will go down with his whole family.

Jean would start dating an old woman who was landlord's wife, she was very old to be dating a little man of Jean's age and calibre, but Jean would never care about age, all he cared was calming his desires, when landlord heard of this, he would try convincing Fauna to have sex with her instead as a revenge for what Jean and his wife have done. Fauna was not an easy woman to convince to do such bad behaviors but she would agree eventually because, Jean has hurt her so much and a lot of times, it was difficult for her to edure and torelate so, she opened her legs to welcome the biggest mistakes of her life.

Fauna decided to sleep with landlord who was much more older than his age, he was approximately to be two times her age. He was on his early 50s while Fauna was on her middle 20s. That revenge was a perfect one because once Ms. Landlord heard about her husband sleeping with her tenant (Fauna), she could never let that go so easily, she had to put witchcraft into action and decided to bewitch Fauna that she won't be attractive to any man, any more, but as a reminder, Fauna's father Mr. Mnik was a medicine man or simply, a witch doctor though people of his village would accuse him of witchcraft actions, means Ms. Landlord's witchcraft could never affect her instead, it affected one of his kids, Joe.

In contrary, when Jean heard all about Landlord and Fauna all he could do was insulting and beating Fauna as an animal.

As people say, tasting once finished a pot, Fauna had tasted sweetness of sex from other men apart from Jean, so she suddenly changed from a very honest and good wife into a harlot-like wife, she changed really bad to the extent of having sex with church's head pastor, luckily little Joe had witnessed everything that have been happening between her mother, Fauna and Pastor and without giving a second thought or atleast having matured senses of what will happen if he says that, only thinking of presents he would be getting after reporting that fraud to his father, he went on yelling everything that was between Mother (Fauna) and Pastor, as far as I can remember, I have never witnessed someone beaten as bad as Fauna that evening. Joe had started a fresh war he did not realise because of his age and low maturity he had at that time.

Fauna hated little Joe so much from the moment little boy carelessly has told Jean matters which were out of his concerns which had shaken her marriage, he could be called 'Mumbeya' (Mumbeya is a swahili slang of a person telling things that are not his or her concerns or without permitted).

Fauna mistakes had given Jean a clear chances of show Fauna what he really is made of, on a broad daylight. He once went out dating a widow who was a primary teacher having two kids older than his own children, indicating that; even that lady was much more older than Jean, he would not care about age all he cared about is that he atleast had someone to have sex with, and he took her in as a second wife. Her name was called Mwl. Esth.

To that stage, of daily insults, beatings, torture and torments, finally on 2008, Fauna would not see her place inside Jean's heart and life what she had to do was running away from that kind of miserable life.

Fun fact about Fauna's running away was that; she tried convincing his son Cyfford who was only three years old about running away but Cyfford refused, he really loved his father at that time since he was the last born of Jean and Fauna. Fauna decided to run away all by herself without knowing that she was carrying Jean's daughter in her stomach who was later on called Anna and that was the last known time Jean ever saw Fauna directly.

****

After Fauna's departure, children had no one to look them so Jean had to take in another woman as his wife to look after his little children at times he would be at work and that's when Verona hoped in.

Mwl. Esth was still considered Jean's wife though Jean had started loosing love on her and as a grown up she saw that coming and she had to dodge a coming shame to such a grown-up and self respecting woman, sho she moved far from Bimulo and Jean's family and was never ever heard again.

But, before Mwl. Esth had to go to unknown far place, alot of things to remember happened and I must let you know them too, but they will be on the next chapter.

Downfall

As I promised on the previous chapter, I have to let you know all that happened before Mwl. Esth's departure and what was the real cause behind her departure.

Mwl. Esth was really a cool woman whoha have had sweated enough providing for her two children all by herself, so getting a man who was willing to take her in as a wife was really encouraging and she could never play with that chance not only Jean but Jean's children loved her very much because sge was a caring and loving mother who knew how to handle things wisely and since she was a teacher, nothing seemed difficult on her side. But, Fauna's departure and Verona's arrival was a thorn to her feelings because Jean would eventually run for a new woman in the house as one of swahili proverbs states; kipya kinyemi ingawa kidonda, (translated as, new is loved and welcomed even if it hurst).

Jean once asked his elder sons on who was better between Verona and Mwl. Esth, Joe chose Mwl. Esth but Frankie chose his favourite, Verona.

Verona was a fierce woman because she would fight anyone who would dare to take his husband but since Mwl. Esth was a kind, educated and matured woman, she could never allow verona get into her nerves so, the fight was never there. Verona was a very brilliant wicked woman so, she had started fire under her feet without her knowledge and that fire would cause time to time misunderstandings between herself and Jean and lastly the only option was leaving the town to neves seen again.

****

Verona who was a bartender when Jean came across, she was a white, fat and had a well built body as Fauna's, she had already had borne two daughters at a time Jean took her in as his wife means, she have had a productive marriage before Jean. She moved in to Jean with her youngest daughter called Soffie, who was only two years old at that time.

It is very hard to explain about Verona's personality because she changed gradually based on the current situation that's why she is the only wife of Jean who stayed longer than any other Jean's wives. Verona would be a cool woman at times but became a very wicked woman at times, so she is very hard to explain but I think you will try to understand and judge her on your own perspectives as we go on.

Verona loved all the kids equally and would never abandon any other child because of any reason but she later on changed when she had he first son, Freeman. At this stage, she had started caring about her own child, even Soffie was treated the same as other children even though she was of her own.

Joe had a previous bad record of being 'mumbeya' a time he told his father about Fauna's wrongdoings with Pastor, but that story turned Joe to be a source of family's chaos. Joe was made to look bad to both family members, relatives and neighbors means any Jean's wife had known that story before even getting all of family members' names, Verona too had seen Joe in a bad angle even before knowing him well. Jean had lit-up that fire severally as he used Joe, his son as a scapegoat whenever was asked on who said those words or who is your witness, so Joe had a bad name in and out of family but he could do nothing about that.

The first person Verona hated in Jean's house was Joe, (a hate with no proper reason) an innocent child turned the worst of Jean's children, He sometimes had to defend himself from Jean's wives who came in with a common enemy who deep inside needed a mother, needed to be loved and cared.

Not all bartenders are the same but I'm really sorry to say this, some bartenders may behave really worse than streets' bitches and think of it as kind of life a bartender should have, firstly, they think a bartender should be kind of a harlot, a bartender should be drunkard and a bartender should have all bad behaviours you know. Since Verona was from that same work before Jean had taken her, she had started adopting kind of that stupid lifestyle, not so long she started having sex with her own brothers-in-law neighbors, men she never knew even people whom she considered parents simply because she was used to be with a large number of men when she was a bartender and now, living with only Jean a busy man was really tiresome for her. She had to fire her hidden litter.

"After a game-done match, results are inevitable, either a win, draw or a loss", Verona lost her match because until she realized the effects of her dirty actions, she was already too late for that because she was now a HIV/AIDS victim (HIV stands for Human immunodeficiency Virus, and AIDS stands for Acquired Immune Deficiency Syndrome), the most fierce and scarry viral disease with no cure that

everyone fears.
Before Verona had acquired HIV/AIDS he had two sons with Jean, Freeman and Cen, Freeman had the exact looks of Jean and Jean had no doubt asking if he was his blood child but Cen looked much more like his mother and as per Verona's cheating behaviours, Jean never believed completely that Cen is of his own fresh, not only Jean and close people had suggested that Jean looked much more like one of Jean's younger brother called Tomsaba.
For years, Jean lived with a deep-inside hatred towards Tomsaba because he had slept with his wife and maybe, Cen was a biological son to Tomsaba.
When Verona had played with her lucky charm, Jean went on to marry another ego-drunk teacher who was his niece, so this female teacher whom Jean is about to take in as his wife was to be a second teacher Jean has married after Mwl. Esth and a second niece he has married right after Fauna, she was celled Happy.
Since Happy was a selfish and egoistic mother she could never stay along with the rest of Jean's family, she had to move away from that crowded family and lived all by herself, luckily she would visit her bank account each month to fill up her pockets, that gave her wings to live like a queen.
Happy did not do great things either good or bad to cherish or hate but she is very much remembered when she fetched Innocent, Aggie and Jean's outcast son whom he refused and openly said he was never his son. At times they were living together he taught Innocent alot of things indluding good behavior towards his elders. Happy found her way out and had gone away from Bimulo and Jean too, right after she was fired from her teaching job. She had

only one daughter with Jean, her name is Precii.

Jean had tasted how changing women was like and he thought with only money, one could get any number of women he wishes, of any size, any color at any time. Jean had slowly started wearing Mr. Mara's shoes, he could not consider woman a wife and a family keeper, but a luxury property.

He now reached the worst stage of polygamy. He thought he could remind himself of old days, he snitched a married woman, a certain teacher's beloved wife, simply because he was much more richer than fifty teachers combined, he started to bully weak people. He always lamented about how weak and helpless he was to be bullied and harassed back at Kyawaza village and swore not to bully anyone if he happen to be stronger than anyone, his words turned against him, not too long he was too strong to be held lightly, he had become a very fierce oppressor compared to none of those oppresed him in Kyawaza. He once was insulted by a drunkard man, he went on beating up the whole of that man's family starting with his old innocent mother, sisters, brothers even little children and law did not see him because they were blinded by bribery.

A woman he snitched from a teacher was named Theresa whom they lasted only few years before she had to departure. Teresa had a very good sexy built body reaching a stage that people would accuse her of using cosmetics to boost her physique because on one could ever believe if a moderate woman would have that sexy physique, though I think, she was blessed maybe, none knows.

Theresa had to go away too because she once was beaten with no proper reason. She only had one daughter with Jean called Jan born on 2018.

Jean's wives could never settle, understand and love one another because each one of them had her own purpose of being there.

Jean stupid action of taking somebody's wife (Theresa) whom he didn't even last with, had closed alot of fortune doors because people started hating him and had started talking on his back because he was now on the highest level of bullying people and people would never hold that back. Simply, taking somebody's wife was ten steps down on his doom's staircase.

Jean went on too far by convincing and leeping with his own sisters in law, he once convinced and slept with Carl's wife, reminded that Carl was both Jean's nephew and a brother to Fauna means he washis brother in law too, not only Carl, Jean went on sleeping several times with Merr, Tomsaba's beloved wife simply because Tomsaba had slept with his wife, Verona. Tomsaba and Carl never loved Jean again bevause he had reached a final stage of being torelated.

What a shame for a brother to sleep with wives of his younger brothers, he made the community not to either love, respect or trust him anymore.

****

The real Jean's doom was still on it's way coming into his life at the highest speed, and unknowingly, he was eagerly waiting for it and welcomed it very warmly to settle into his own realm.

That doom was named Helleda, a young town girl, as long as she was defined young, she was actually beautiful, she was on her late 20s almost to Joe and Frankie's age, and almost a half of Jeans age since Jean was on his early 40s. She was a bartender too, the same work Verona had done,

Jean had never tasted alcohol in his life and he was never expected to be a drunkard but he got two of his wives on bar, how was that?

Jean had made alot of friends who would help him with connections and as friends, he would always take them to bars, groceries or night clubs in order for him to gain their attention and support because, "Faeces is bee's best gift, not honey. " Jean would too go to bars because they are only places where meat would be available plenty everyday and every time, since he was a good meet monger, why would he not be present to cheer the parties?

At first sight I met Helleda (Jean's future wife), was on a countryside village where they (Jean and her) had gone to have enough space for their conversations and so on, since she was not an official Jean's wife at that time, they loved to be far away on mountainous villages to keep themselves far away from people's sights and to enjoy that little vacation, they never went with their cars (Helleda had no car at that time, I refer to only Jean). That evening Jean caught cold on the mountains and a quick help was reaching me, he could not call someone else because of the bomb he will be making for himself. I could drive at that time because I had driving classes starting on my late 10s, and I quickly reached and fetched them, that's where I firstly met Jean'sdestroyed.

Great Strike

Before Jean had officially brought Helleda at his realm, he had a very prestigious life that was envied by everyone in Bimulo district, he was among the top richest people in Bimulo, he had dozens of cars, he had given a car, business and a house to each of his wives, he had invested in business, he had alot of piece of lands in and outside of Bimulo, he was on the last stages of preparations to finish his own hospital and he had zero debts from either people , loan sharks or banks. Additionally, all of his children were studying on expensive private schools where he would pay ten millions of Tanzanian shillings annually as their school fees plus other expenses.

Helleda was brought and Jean had held a secret wedding ceremony at Helleda's home village, he did not invite anyone on the wedding because no one loved Helleda even before they had not lived with her, one could see a bad person, bad sister in law, bad daughter, bad friend and a bad mom on just the fist meeting with Helleda. Since she was the youngest of Jean's wives, she would think she was the most beautiful woman in the whole of Bimulo because rich people are thought to marry beautiful women.

I and other family children were at school (boarding) at a time Helleda was brought in as Jeans wife because she was brought in at the middle of the year. I was on my last year as a high school student at that time when everything started.

As normal as usual, the first thing Helleda heard about Jean's family was Joe's fantasy that had taken place more than fifteen years ago, Joe had made another enemy unwillingly but since he was used to that, it was just normal because they ususally came, hate and lastly departed without knowing that, seriousness this lady came with was unseasonably.

1ST MISSION

Helleda's first mission she had to accomplish was to make sure that she remains as the only wife to Jean, she had to get all of Jean's wives kicked out of their houses (they were three at a time, Happy [though living a bit far from Jean's houses], Theresa and Verona). She had arranged her plots so well and had choosen a weapon to use against themselves, that was the dumbest of all, Verona, as I said before, though verona seemed to be dumb but she was very tricky and wise in terms of starting a fight and finding faults at others. Helleda left all the work to Verona and without even thinking about herself, Verona had raised chaos that would see every remained Jean's wife run away even without asking for divorce and lastly she would think that the work was done but it actually was her turn to leave the house, what a dumpster she was.

2ND MISSION

On the second mission Helleda wanted to accomplish was to kick out all of Jean's relatives. Jean's was never a cold blooded human, he would always welcome anyone especially his relatives in need, his relatives were the great help to Jean's investments, though he would get into conflicts with them sometimes like Tombaya's case (refer the last chapter) he would forgive them and life had to go on, they would have better lives and he would add something to his fortune. Helleda thought Jean's relatives would disturb her if Jean died, she only thought about inheritance and fortune.

She would not directly tell Jean to kick them out so she had a well planned plot too, she would sexually provoke Jean's relatives and turn her back to tell Jean that, some of his relatives wanted to sleep with her but she refused, and without a second thought Jean kicked them away. She then adviced Jean to sell some of his properties to focus on only few properties they could handle, she had to give him alot of bra bra explanations for Jean to agree. We really don't know what she had given Jean because he would agree to any suggestion she was giving to him.

Selling his own properties after agreeing to Helleda's advise such as site cars and shops found alot of his own relatives lost their jobs and they had to look for a new life away from Jean, Helleda succeeded on her second mission.

3RD MISSION

Dispite all successful battles she won, Helleda still wanted more, she tried the most difficult task, she tried to find a way that Jean would kick his own children out of their own home, she started by advising Jean on not to spend too much on children education, with a reason that; even children who had studied on normal schools had a better lives than some of people went to private and expensive schools, she gave alot of silly examples of people in the society and lastly all the kids were taken away from expensive to free government schools.

Since she was now near them, she would easily see kids' faults and reported everything that was happening (only bad deeds actually), Jean as if evil spirit had entered him, had started hating his own kids to the extent of comparing them to dogs and would never give them a chance to explain themselves.

Frankie had to run away from home, he thought he had run away from troubles but he had given a winning card to Helleda.

Helleda had to focus on Joe who was a high school graduate waiting to go to University, a story Helleda never wanted because if these kids get proper education and become proffesionals, she would be in trouble on future.

Joe was never an easy opponent to deal with but she got his weak point, 'anger', she would provoke him on something he never wanted to hear or do and out of anger, Joe would insult, start chaos and speak the unspeakable, all she would do was calling the witnesses and sort out points she wanted to hear. The rest was a story.

****

Jean's wealthy and fortune had started fading away slowly, but he had to keep on listening to her beloved Helleda, who advised him on going for a government post, she would tell him to run for election as one of the candidates to become Bimulo constituency's member of parliament. She then advised him on borrowing a large sum from banks and roan sharks to help him run his political campaigns.

Time of election came and Jean was defeated badly, he mabaged to only get two votes out of all votes, even his own friends could not vote for him, that's when he realized that all those noise of people cheering, were not for him but for those precious papers he was having inside his pockets.

Jean had entered a miserable life, he even though one of

his past wives had bewitched him or brought bad lucky into his family, he started living a miserable life, he would bring a couple of witch doctors each months to make up things for him but he was too late, every mornings were his fading and evenings were his dimming times.

Jean had sold all of his cars, investments and properties, all children had run away. He was now rich of unpaid debts. He always run away from his debtors. He was simpy a mess.

Helleda have one daughter with Jean, and she still lives in Jean's house, she fought bravery to get everything but she eventually had to witness everything fading away right infront of her eyes, she sometimes have to stay hungry because there's no food she sometimes have to stay in a darker house at night because he hasn't paid electricity bills.

Where Did everyone Go

Let's see a summary of the current lives of some of the main Characters in our beautiful novel.

JEAN

Jean still lives to date, he is still a healthy middle aged man in his early 40s. He is still married to the same young wicked woman called Helleda, even though his life many not be as great as before, he is still happy and continue trying again and again thinking maybe one day he may a hieve something great as he had achieved before and return to the realm he thinks is his. Jean has never given a second thought on his behaviors, he is is still as fresh as always on hitting on young or even matured street women.

HELLEDA

Dispite all the things Helleda has cause the family to pass through, the losses of family members and wealthy, Helleda has never changed her plan and has no plans to, she is still wicked, short tempered and selfish as always that she even wishes to have everything under her control whether Jeans lives or dies. I could never understand her neither. For a woman to have such behaviors as Helleda, there must be a hidden agenda hehind all that, I guess I might come up with Helleda's story when I get in touch with it all.

MR. MARA

Mr. Mara who may be the center of this beautiful story is

still in Kyawaza village, healthy and still live to his fullest, though he is too much older on his late 80s he still marries to date and have a large number of wives as before (though many of them might be reduced because of unavoidable reasons such as deaths and divorces) He is still aggressive as his youth times so if anyone dares to make him angry thinking that he is too much old to handle him, he is lying all by himself.

JOE

Since Joe was dumped for a numerous times now, he decided to part ways with his father and family and look into other possible ways to survive, he is now living a simple but sure life in one if bot the largest city in Tanzaland since he would never wish returning on the same places as his parents and grandparents, he is very much afraid being like one of them.

Joe has not married and has got jo plans to marry, he mostly wishes to have lots of money and fame.

FRANKIE

Nobody has ever understood this giant kid, he is neither good nor bad, he really loves his family and would actually wish to settle down with them, he loves family unit but dince it is disintegrated, he is unable to do anything about that. Acter his longer runaways, he actually returned to his father and he is helping jim in his works, what a great kid.

FAUNA

After a controversial divorce, Fauna went on living a bachelor's life with his one daughter, Anna who she had with Jean, though Cyfford went on living with him because he could not his future on Jean's and Helleda's home.

AGGIE

Aggie has always hived her life, hidden and running like a

wild rat, she has never settled down, she is always in the run, he life can not be understood even by people who thinks to be closer ro her

CYFFORD

Cyfford returned to his birth mother, Fauna to live with her and her young sister, Anna. As Joe, Cyfford could never see any bright future of him under Jean's territories so he peacefully had to make his own way and see if he could make it a better future for himself.

INNOCENT

He has always had a complicated life of following wherever it flows, he never have his own decisions, at the end Cyfford left him at home where he is still at to date, he has been turned a working machine, he does all the house chores starting with general cleanliness to cooking of food and utensils.

VERONA

After a decade of struggling, torments, beatings and sufferings, she lastly freed herself from Jean's territories and started her fresh life as a bartender living in the same city as Joe though they have never had a chance to meet or come across one another. Verona still looks for a better life to one day take her two little sons, Freman and Cen and live together with them.

FREMAN AND CEN

These two little and innocent kids still live under their father's roof sharing it with their wicked step mother, Helleda though since Innocent, their brother has joined them at home, they are somewhat relieved, they still wait and hope that, maybe there comes a day that any good and peaceful life they had may come on again.

HAPPY AND PRECII

Happy is living with her little angel daughter, Precii in Manza Town, (one of the cities the whole story started) whom she had with Jean, though she has no any known hood life, she can still take care of her child, though she has always cry for a help from Jean.

TERESA AND JAN

Mama Jane got a new job the moment she got away from Jean's hands, she is now living a good life and nursing her little daughter, Jane she too had with Jean.

TOMSABA, MERRIE AND FAMILY

Tommamba could never settle down the disputes and misunderstandings he had with his brother, Jean, the onky solution he could think of was, selling the house, taking his family and leave Bimulo Town because he could no longer bear shame that was coming right infront of his eyes.

CARL, WIVES AND FAMILY

Carl has never been afraid of Jean, his nephew and at the same time, brother in law. He still lives in Bimulo very close to Jean's neighborhood. Carl forgave his wife whom they still live together till today though he actually added another one to maintain discipline inside the house.

MWL. ESTH AND FAMILY

For decades now, no one has ever heard anything from MWl. Esth or any of her kids, she went on living a very quiet life very far from Bimulo and Jean.

Morals

"Either good or bad, they both teach", one of my teachers used to use that old saying, as we approach on the peak of our beautiful story I would like to add whenever I learned from this life-long story and I hope you can too add whatever you think is helpful and will help teach the society.

• Despite everything, Family comes first

• No one is above the law

• Polygamy is not a solution to a man's problems, facing and solving them with one patner will help you avoid other unnecessary troubles

• Anger is not always an answer

• Courtship is a very important period to any couple before marriage.

• Early marriages should be stopped by all means

• Children are blessings and not burdens

• If you want to make world a better palce, take a look at yourself and make a change

• Female children are very much equal and sometimes better than male children, they should be educated and treated as children not as female children.

• Hardworking pays

• Lastly, fathers abandoning their families, mothers throwing away their kids and step parents torturing children should be reported and severely punished otherwise they should be cursed.

• Money come and go, humanity is the most important of all.

If you have reached at this point, I hope you have read and enjoyed this dramatic true story. All I can say to you is; thank you so much for being with me fom the start of this beautiful story till now…See you on the next novel……"

www.ingramcontent.com/pod-product-compliance
Lightning Source LLC
LaVergne TN
LVHW050421160726
843469LV00041B/1173

* 9 7 8 9 3 5 6 1 0 5 0 6 5 *